MASTER THIS!

Guitar

Seb Wesson

PowerKiDS
press™
New York

Published in 2011 by The Rosen Publishing Group Inc.
29 East 21st Street, New York, NY 10010

Copyright © 2011 Wayland/
The Rosen Publishing Group, Inc.

First Edition

Senior Editor: Claire Shanahan
Produced by Tall Tree Ltd.
Editor, Tall Tree: Jon Richards
Designer: Jonathan Vipond

Library of Congress Cataloging-in-Publication Data

Wesson, Seb.
  Guitar / by Seb Wesson. -- 1st ed.
      p. cm. -- (Master this!)
  Includes index.
  ISBN 978-1-61532-599-3 (library binding)
  ISBN 978-1-61532-606-8 (paperback)
  ISBN 978-1-61532-607-5 (6-pack)
  1. Guitar--Methods--Juvenile. I. Title.
  MT801.G8W47 2011
  787.87'193--dc22
                                            2009045763

Manufactured in China
CPSIA Compliance Information: Batch #WAS0102PK: For Further Information
contact Rosen Publishing, New York, New York at 1-800-237-9932

Photographs
All photographs taken by Michael Wicks, except: t-top, b-bottom, l-left, r-right, c-center
2 Dreamstime.com/Vladislav Lebedinskiy, 5t Stephen Hiird/Reuters/Corbis, 5b Dreamstime.com/Nexus7, 6l Dreamstime.com/Vladislav Lebedinskiy, 7l Dreamstime.com/Magomed Magomedagaev, 7r Dreamstime.com/Duane Ellison, 8tr Dreamstime.com/Robert Spriggs, 8bl Corbis, 9b Dreamstime.com/Andrea Leone, 13tl Dreamstimecom/Magda Moiola, 15tr Tim Wimborne/Reuters/Corbis, 17br Michael Ochs Archives/Corbis, 26tr Joe Giron/Corbis, 28 Josh Armstrong/The Christian Science Monitor via Getty Images, 29t istockphoto.com

Disclaimer
In preparation of this book, all due care has been exercised with regard to the advice, activities, and techniques depicted. The publishers regret that they can accept no liability for any loss or injury sustained. When learning a new activity, it is important to get expert tutelage and to follow a manufacturer's instructions.

Acknowledgements
The publishers would like to thank Chad Brown, Lucy Pisapia, and Tom Jordan for their help with this book.

Contents

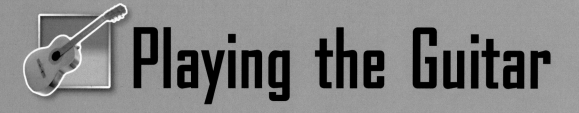

Playing the Guitar

The guitar is one of the most exciting musical instruments you can learn to play. It works wonderfully when it is played with someone who is singing or other instruments, or when it is played as a solo instrument.

Played by All

The guitar can be played in a wide range of musical styles, or genres, from classical to rock to jazz. Anyone can learn to play the guitar at any age, whether they are left- or right-handed. The positions described in this book are for right-handed players—you will need to reverse them if you are left-handed.

Mastering the guitar takes a lot of practice because it requires a great deal of coordination between your left and right hands.

*Mastering the guitar can pave the way to some exciting experiences. Here, Dave Grohl of the Foo Fighters plays a guitar **solo** in front of a huge crowd during a concert in London, UK, in 2007.*

Guitar Heroes

There are many famous rock and pop guitar players. Eric Clapton and Jimi Hendrix popularized blues and rock guitar in the 1960s. Eric Clapton is still performing today to enormous crowds around the world. Brian May from Queen and Eddie Van Halen from Van Halen took rock guitar into the 1970s and 1980s, and bands such as Green Day and the Foo Fighters have brought guitar playing into the twenty-first century. All these bands and players have different musical styles and use the guitar in different ways.

History

Musical instruments similar to the guitar have been around for more than 5,000 years. However, different numbers of strings were used in instruments, such as the **oud** with 11 strings. The modern, six-stringed classical guitar first appeared in Seville, Spain, in the 1850s.

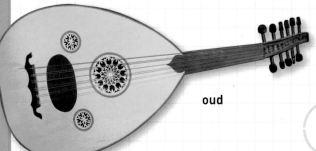

oud

Types of Guitar

There are two types of guitar used in modern music; the **acoustic** guitar and the electric guitar. Although the principles and techniques of playing them are the same, they can be used to create very different sounds.

Vibrating Strings

All guitars have strings that are plucked to make them **vibrate**. This vibrating produces the notes. Most guitars have six strings, each of a different thickness. The thinner the string, the higher the note it produces. You can also change the **pitch** of a note, by placing your fingers on the fretboard.

headstock

nut

tuning keys

fretboard

acoustic guitar

fret

sound hole

bridge

strings

waist curve

body

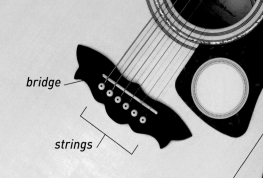

Fretboard

The fretboard is divided up into different areas using raised bars called frets. The areas between the frets refer to different notes. By putting your finger on the string near a fret, you are making the string shorter, and the shorter you make a string, the higher the note it produces.

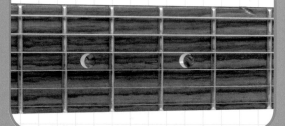

Making It Louder

Electric and acoustic guitars differ in how they **amplify** the notes, or make them louder. Acoustic guitars have a large, hollow body. The air inside the body vibrates with the strings, making the notes louder when they come out of the sound hole. Electric guitars have electric **pickups**, which detect the vibrations of the strings (see below).

tuning keys tighten and loosen the strings to tune the guitar

headstock provides fixing points for the ends of the strings and the tuning keys

fretboard

fret

electric guitar

Top Tip

When buying a new guitar, you should find something you are comfortable with when you play it. You may like the look of a pointy guitar, but it will not sit as comfortably as a classically shaped model.

How Pickups Work

Magnets in the pickups create a **magnetic field**. The pickups detect the vibrations of the strings in this magnetic field and convert them into electrical signals. These signals are sent to an amplifier (see pages 8–9), where they are made louder.

pickups

bridge

tremolo arm temporarily alters the pitch of the notes

volume controls

body

jack to connect guitar to amplifier

Other Equipment

In addition to the guitar itself, there are a few other pieces of equipment you will need. This equipment will help you tune, hold, amplify, and strum your guitar correctly.

Accessories

A guitar strap is essential when playing in live situations since it will help you to hold the guitar while standing up (see pages 10–11). It should be adjustable so that it holds your guitar at the correct height. If you are sitting down to play, then a foot rest will raise your foot and stop the guitar from slipping off, and a music stand will hold any sheet music at eye level.

Using a Pick

pick

Picks (plectrums) are used to pick the strings. They come in a variety of thicknesses, but usually, you should use a thinner pick for strumming chords and a thicker one for playing a tune.

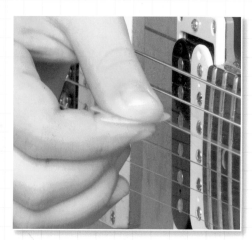

Hold the pick between the first finger and thumb of your strumming hand—if you are right-handed, this is your right hand.

Amplifier

The amplifier, or amp, contains electronic parts and a speaker that amplify, or make louder, the sounds from your electric guitar. You will also need cables to carry signals from the guitar output jack to the amplifier or to an electric guitar tuner (see below). These cables do not carry electricity to power the guitar and amp, but they carry the electrical signals created by the pickups (see pages 6–7).

*Amps allow you to control the volume of the notes, making them louder or quieter. They also allow you to control how much **bass** and **treble** your guitar sounds make.*

Electric Tuner

An electric tuner detects the vibrations of each string and shows you whether that string is playing the right note (in tune) or not. You can then turn the tuning keys (see page 7) on the guitar to tighten or loosen the string to tune it (see page 17).

Holding the Guitar

You can play the guitar sitting down or standing up. In general, acoustic music is played in a sitting position, but electric music, such as rock and pop, is played standing up, using a strap.

right arm should rest on top of the guitar's body

left hand should support the guitar's neck

When sitting to play an acoustic guitar, the waist curve of the guitar should rest on your right thigh.

legs should be level and not slope toward the floor

Sitting

Guitarists who play classical music tend to keep their legs wider while holding the guitar neck higher.

Standing

A good height to position your guitar when standing is a little lower than you would have it in the sitting position. Start in a sitting position and stand up, holding the guitar where it is. You can then see how much you need to loosen or tighten your strap. Some guitarists, such as Slash from Guns N' Roses, hold the guitar very low, but others, such as Johnny Borel from Razorlight, hold it much higher. There is no set way to hold your guitar—just do what works best for you.

guitar strap

guitar body is held a little lower than when sitting

egs are straight but he knees are not ocked

Hand on the Neck

Your left hand should be positioned so that it can move along the neck easily, without you having to strain too hard. You should avoid gripping the neck too hard, keeping your fingers soft and relaxed instead.

fingers should be able to reach all of the strings without straining

Chords and Strumming

A major part of playing the guitar includes playing chords. A chord is a group of notes that is played together at the same time.

Finger Work

The individual notes of the chord are made by positioning the finger tips of the left hand on the fretboard in the correct positions. When placing the fingers on the fretboard, it is important that they are close to the relevant fret, otherwise they will not sound the note correctly. The right hand can then strum all or some of the strings to sound the notes.

To sound a note correctly, you should put your finger on the string next to the relevant fret. Here, a guitarist has put his index finger up against a fret of the thickest string.

Strumming Techniques

To strum the first chord, the hand holding the pick is held above the thickest string.

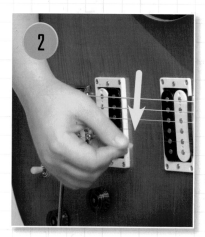

The hand is brought down quickly so that it hits, or plucks, each of the strings on the way down.

To play the next chord, the pick hand is brought upward, plucking each of the strings again.

The guitar's six strings each have their own note. The thickest string plays the lowest-sounding note, and the thinnest string the highest. The strings, from the thickest to the thinnest, play the following notes: E, A, D, G, B, E.

Setting the Mood

Chords can really set the mood of what you are playing, depending on what **key** they are in. For example, if the music is in a **major** key, then the chord may sound happy, but if it is a **minor** key, it can sound sad. Chords are used to create a musical layer in a song, over which a solo instrument will be played or a **vocalist** will sing. Chords can even be broken down into an arpeggio. This is when the notes of a chord are played one after the other, instead of at the same time (see pages 22–23).

A chord box is a way of writing down a chord to show how it is played on the guitar. At the top, there is an "0" to show that the string should be played without any fingers on a fret—this is known as "open"—or an "X" to show that you should not play that string (see the chords on page 19).

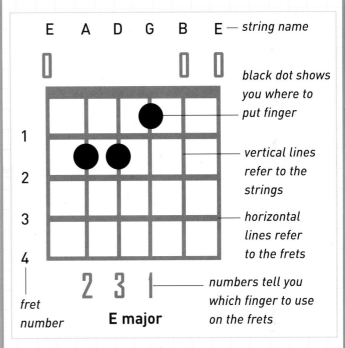

E major

fret number — black dot shows you where to put finger — string name — vertical lines refer to the strings — horizontal lines refer to the frets — numbers tell you which finger to use on the frets

These are the finger positions for the chord box shown above. The fingers of the fret hand are numbered from one for the index finger to four for the little finger.

Scales and Picking

Scales are individual notes arranged in order from the lowest note to the highest and back down again. Scales are used for many things in music, such as exercises to warm up your fingers. You will also find that most tunes are based on scales.

Top Tip

You should change the strings on your guitar regularly to stop them breaking or rusting. Your guitar teacher can show you how to replace them.

One at a Time

Unlike chords, where all the notes are played at the same time, notes in a scale are played one at a time, using a technique called alternate picking. This involves striking the string down for the first note, then upward for the second note, then down for the next note, and so on.

Alternate Picking

Hold the pick above the string you wish to play and then strike it downward to pick the first note.

Bring the pick upward to pick the string and change the finger position on the frets to play a note with a different pitch.

Playing Tabs

Guitar tablature, or tab for short, is a simple way of recording information for guitarists. You can use it to read scales and chords as well as complete pieces of music, without having to learn how to read musical notation (see pages 16–19).

Tabs use a system of lines for the strings and numbers to show which fret the fingers should be placed on (see below).

Star File

THE EDGE
Rock Legend

David Evans, also known as The Edge, is part of Irish rock band U2. He is famous for his simple tunes, or melodies, and distinctive chiming guitar sound, which he creates using special sound effects. He has played with U2 since they formed 30 years ago, and has created rock classics such as *City of Blinding Lights* and *Vertigo.*

How to Read Guitar Tabs

The top line represents the thinnest string, which plays the highest note, and the bottom line represents the thickest string, which plays the lowest note. The letters on the side represent the names of the notes of each of the strings (see page 13). The numbers that appear on the strings represent the frets you should hold down. As with the chord box, "0" means that the string should be played "open," with no fingers on a fret.

Guitarists read the tabs from left to right, playing the fret indicated by the first number before moving onto the next number to the right, and so on. The guitar tabs featured here are for the scales C major and A minor.

letters represent string notes *horizontal lines represent strings* *numbers indicate which fret to play*

```
e | - - - - - - - - - - - - - - - - - - - - - |
b | - - - - - - - - - - - - - 0 - 1 - - - - - |
g | - - - - - - - - - 0 - 2 - - - - - - - - - |
d | - - - 0 - 2 - 3 - - - - - - - - - - - - - |
a | - 3 - - - - - - - - - - - - - - - - - - - |
e | - - - - - - - - - - - - - - - - - - - - - |
```
C major

```
e | - - - - - - - - - - - - - - - - - - - - - |
b | - - - - - - - - - - - - - - - - - - - - - |
g | - - - - - - - - - - - - - - - 0 - 2 - - - |
d | - - - - - - - 0 - 2 - 3 - - - - - - - - - |
a | - 0 - 2 - 3 - - - - - - - - - - - - - - - |
e | - - - - - - - - - - - - - - - - - - - - - |
```
A minor

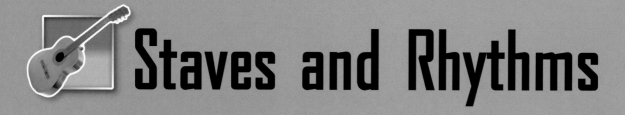

Staves and Rhythms

As well as using guitar tablature and chord boxes, you can read music using musical notation. This is a system of dots that are positioned on a group of lines called a staff.

Guitar Music

At the start of each line of music is a symbol called a **clef**. This shows you how high or low the notes on the staff are to be played. There are several different clefs, but music for the guitar is written using the treble clef. This means that the notes on the lines of the staff are, from lowest-pitched to highest, E, G, B, D, and F. The spaces on the treble clef staff are, from lowest to highest, F, A, C, and E. Put together, the notes make up the entire musical alphabet (see pages 18–19) using the letters A to G. Notes above or below the staff sit on small lines known as ledger lines.

This guitarist is reading sheet music, which contains several staves of musical notation, one on top of the other.

The Staff

You can remember the line notes of the treble clef with the phrase "Every Good Boy Does Fine," and the space notes spell out the word "FACE."

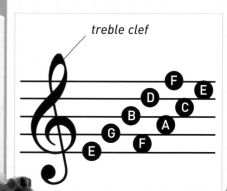

treble clef

Rhythms

As well as the notes and pitches, you need to know the right **rhythms** in order to play a piece of music. Music is divided up into bars, and a simple bar of music usually contains four beats. These beats are called **quarter notes** and one beat equals one quarter note. The number of beats in a bar is shown by the **time signature**, which consists of two numbers that are written just after the clef.

Bar Beats

In this case, there are four quarter notes in a bar, as shown by the "four-four" time signature. Each bar is divided by a bar line. Different symbols are used to show notes of different lengths. For example, two quarter notes, or beats, equal a **half note**. Two half notes equal a **whole note**.

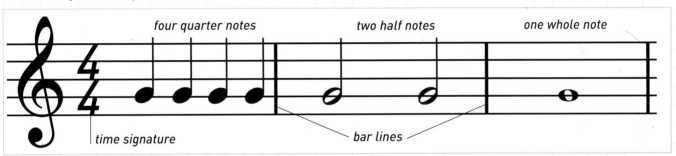

four quarter notes　　　　two half notes　　　　one whole note

time signature　　　　　　bar lines

Tuning

To tune the guitar strings so that they play the correct notes, you can either use an electric guitar tuner (see page 9) or you can use your ear. Play the fifth fret of the thickest string (E) and it will sound the note that the string next to it should play (A). Tighten or loosen that string until it plays the same note. You can work up the guitar strings in this way, always playing the fifth fret of the string before the one you want to tune. One exception is the G string, where you have to play the fourth fret to sound the right note.

Star File

DJANGO REINHARDT
Gypsy Master

Django Reinhardt was born in France on the January 23, 1910. As a young man, his hand was injured in a fire and this prevented him from using two of his fingers on the fretboard. However, this did not stop him from developing an amazingly fast playing technique. He went on to invent the lively style of guitar music known as gypsy jazz.

The Musical Alphabet

As you play higher and higher pitched notes, the letters in the musical alphabet are repeated again and again. The jump from one A to the next A (or any other two notes with the same letter) is called an **octave**.

Sharps and Flats

Each octave jump is split into eight notes and in between most of these, there are other notes known as sharps (#) and flats (b). The gap between two notes is an **interval**, and the smallest interval used in music, for example, from A to A#, is a **half step** or **semitone**. An interval of two half steps, from A to B, is a **whole step** or **tone**.

Notes and Frets

The entire musical alphabet, with all the sharps and flats looks like this:
A-A#(Bb)-B-C-C#(Db)-E-F-F#(Gb)-G-G#(Ab)-A.
You will notice that a sharp note is the same as the flattened note above it. For example, A# is the same note as Bb. Also, B-C and E-F do not have sharps or flats between them because they are a half step apart. Below is an entire octave of notes, written out as musical notation and as a guitar tab. You will see on the tab that as you play one fret higher, the note rises a half step.

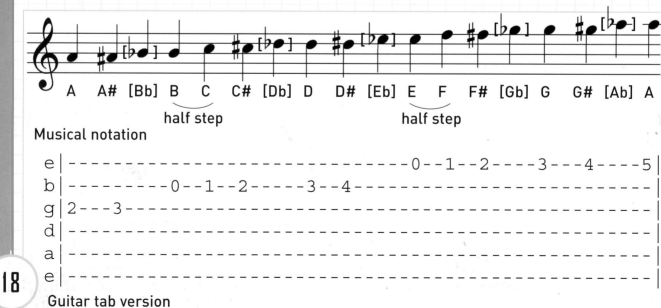

A   A# [Bb] B   C   C# [Db] D   D# [Eb] E   F   F# [Gb] G   G# [Ab] A

half step   half step

Musical notation

```
e|-----------------------------------------------------0--1--2----3---4----5|
b|---------------0--1--2----3--4--------------------------------------------|
g|2---3--------------------------------------------------------------------|
d|------------------------------------------------------------------------|
a|------------------------------------------------------------------------|
e|------------------------------------------------------------------------|
```

Guitar tab version

Using the Notes

Major and minor scales are formed by putting together specific sequences of whole steps and half steps. A major scale uses a certain sequence of whole and half steps. These are: root (starting note and key), whole step, whole step, half step, whole step, whole step, whole step, half step. Using the musical alphabet and starting on the note A, you will get the A major scale and it should look like this: A-B-C#-D-E-F#-G#-A.

Minor scales use a different sequence by lowering the third and sixth notes of the scale by a half step. So an A minor scale would read: A-B-C-D-E-F-G#-A.

Top Tip

To help you visualize the intervals between each of the notes, look at the keyboard of a piano. There are thinner black keys for the sharps and flats between all of the notes except B–C and E–F.

Making Chords

You can also use scales to make chords. Playing the first, third, and fifth notes from a major scale will give you a major chord. For instance, in A major, that would be A-C#-E. Playing the first, third, and fifth notes of a minor scale will give you a minor chord (A-C-E).

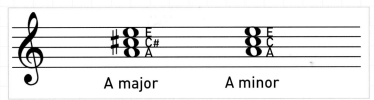

A major   A minor

In musical notation, the notes of a chord are written above each other, as shown here. Now compare these with the chord boxes and photographs shown below.

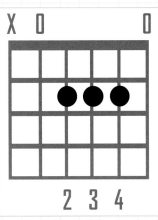

A major

A major

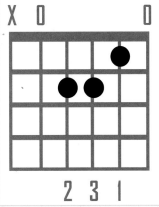

A minor

A minor

Special Effects

There are several techniques you can use to create different effects when you are playing scales, soloing, and **improvising**.

Bending and Slides

Bending strings is a technique that is used across all styles of music. This involves pushing, or "bending," a string so that it plays a higher note.

Slides are a way of getting from one note to another on the same string with a sliding sound effect. You can slide up and down between two notes.

Bending

Play a note using your third finger on the fret, with the other fingers behind it.

Push all your fingers up so they bend the string, making the note sound higher.

Slide

Play a note using your third finger on the fret (although any finger can be used).

Slide finger toward the guitar's body by two frets to play note a whole step higher.

Hammer Ons and Pull Offs

These techniques can be used to give you very smooth-sounding phrases when playing solos on the guitar. Hammer ons require a little bit of force to sound the second note correctly, but they will get easier with practice. Pull offs are the opposite to hammer ons. You can combine the two techniques into a loop, so that a whole string of notes can be made with just a few picks.

Hammer On

Play a note using the first finger on the fretboard.

"Hammer" down a finger two frets nearer the guitar's body to play note a whole step higher.

Pull Off

Place your third finger on the fretboard with your first finger placed two frets down.

Play the first note and pull the third finger away quickly to sound the second note.

Rhythm and Chord Skills

Once you have mastered the basic skills for chords, you can use further techniques that will help you to put chords together to make sequences and to write songs.

Arpeggiating

When you are playing chord sequences, you can strum them in a rhythm, or you could break up the notes in the chord and play them in a sequence. This is called arpeggiating. You can make you own chord sequences up for arpeggiating, too. Play the notes slowly and make sure you let each one ring out.

Finger Style

Classical, folk, and blues guitarists often use their fingers instead of a pick. This allows them to play more than one note at once. It also makes a softer sound since they use the fleshy part of the fingertips rather than a pick.

3

2

1

4

When playing finger style, the fingers and thumb of the picking hand are indicated by the numbers one to four and a "T" for the thumb.

T

Finger Style Sequence

The guitar tab on the right shows a simple arpeggiated chord sequence you can play using **finger style**. The numbers on each string refer to the frets used on that string, and the numbers and letter "T" along the bottom tell you which finger to pick the string with.

```
e|---------|---------|---------|
b|-------1-|-------1-|---------|
g|-----2---|-----0---|-------0-|
d|---2-----|---2-----|-----0---|
a|-0-------|-3-------|---2-----|
e|---------|---------|-3-------|
 |-T-1-2-3-|-T-1-2-3-|-T-1-2-3-|
   A minor    C Major    G major
```

Using a Capo

The guitar capo is a useful tool because it clamps across the six strings of the guitar and allows you to play any open chords but in a different key. This can be very handy if you write your own songs or sing someone else's, but find that the key is too low or high for your voice.

You can move the capo up and down the fretboard in order to find a pitch that best suits you.

Top Tip

When playing finger style, some people, especially classical players, grow their fingernails long. The nails can then be used as individual picks on each finger.

capo

# Advanced Techniques

The techniques shown here will take some time to get right, but mastering them will let you play songs in many different styles.

Tuning Variations

Many guitarists choose to change the way their guitars are tuned and then combine this with other techniques to create individual sounds. Drop D tuning, for example, involves tuning your thickest string down from an E to a D. You will need your electric tuner for this, or you could try playing your fourth or D string and tuning the string down to "match" it (although it will need to be an octave lower). Once you have tuned the string, you can play the three low strings all together. They will make a low, "heavy"-sounding chord. You can then try this on the fifth fret and the third or any other fret of your choice, giving you some more drop D "**power chords**" (see page 25).

Here, the lowest string on a guitar is being tuned to play drop D chords. Although drop D tuning can be used on all types of guitars, it sounds best on electric guitars.

Top Tip

Try drop D chords by fretting the lowest three strings on the first, second, and third frets. Bands such as the Foo Fighters use this technique for heavy rock songs to great effect.

Harmonics

A harmonic is a chimelike note that sounds different from normal guitar notes. It is produced by lightly touching the string, but without actually fretting a note. This does not work on all frets on the guitar, so you need to know which ones to use. The twelfth fret gives you the best and clearest harmonic (see right), although the fifth and seventh frets will also work.

There are also harmonics available on the third and ninth frets, but these are much harder to master. When they are done correctly, you should hear the chimelike sound. Try this on all the six strings on the twelfth fret, then the fifth and seventh frets, too.

Playing Harmonics

Place your second fingertip on top of the twelfth fret of the thickest string.

Pluck that string with a firm downstroke using your pick, and let go of the string with your fret hand as you do so.

Power Chords

Power chords are used a lot in rock and heavy metal music. They are simple to do and can be moved around into different positions almost anywhere on the fretboard to make "riffs" or songs. Bands such as Green Day have used this technique effectively in their songs.

B power chord

D power chord

Putting It Together

In order to write your own songs and play your own solos, you will need to put together the individual skills shown so far. Do not be afraid to experiment—just play what you think sounds good.

Writing Songs

By taking some chords and mixing them around, you should be able to come up with chord sequences. Try them in a different order and keep mixing things up. Eventually, you will come across a sequence you like. This can form the basis of your song, over which you can play a melody.

Star File

KURT COBAIN
Grunge Guitarist

Born April 20, 1967, Kurt Cobain used the guitar to great effect in his songwriting and soloing. He led the band Nirvana during the late 1980s and early 1990s and was also partly responsible for the birth of grunge, a type of music influenced by punk, heavy metal, and indie rock. Despite his death in 1994, he is still an enormous influence on guitarists today.

Chord Sequence

Below are chord boxes and photographs showing a simple chord structure: C major, G major, A minor, and E minor. You can write chord sequences down, so that other guitarists can play them.

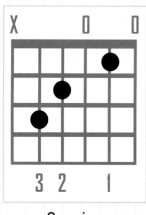

C major

C major

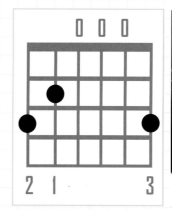

G major

G major

Improvising

Many rock guitarists improvise, or make up, guitar solos during a performance. Improvised guitar solos normally use a scale and change the order and way in which the notes are played. See if you can play the notes from the C major scale shown on pages 14–15 so that they sound good with the chord sequence shown below. There is no right way to play a guitar solo, so just experiment and see what you like, but make sure you have fun!

The chord sequence shown below would look like this: ||:C,,,|G,,,|Am,,,|Em,,,:||
The commas show how many times the chords should be played, and the dots at the start and the end show that the whole sequence should be repeated.

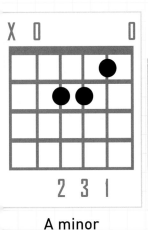

A minor

A minor

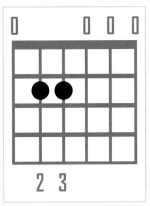

E minor

E minor

Taking It Further

With the help of a good music teacher, you can really learn how to master the guitar. Playing with others is also a great way of improving your guitar skills. You may even go on to form your own band and possibly play gigs.

Finding a Teacher

Your school or your local music store are good places to ask about a suitable guitar teacher. Stores and schools will have the details of local teachers and will be able to tell you if they teach the type of music you are interested in. Some teachers may give lessons only in classical music, for instance, and others might teach rock and blues. However, there are teachers who will cover a little bit of everything and are not limited to just a couple of styles.

The Internet is also great for locating a music teacher near you. It can also be a good source of guitar information, such as tabs and advice on buying guitars and different techniques.

A good guitar teacher will show you correct playing techniques in either one-to-one or group lessons.

These guitarists are jamming. Many of the biggest bands started out with a group of friends playing for fun, just like this.

Turning Pro

To play the guitar for a living, you will have to spend many hours mastering all of its techniques. However, there are plenty of jobs available for professional guitarists. These include teaching music and guitar, working in recording studios, and writing your own music.

Playing with Others

Working with other musicians is a very important part of guitar playing. You should be sympathetic to other musicians and make sure you always listen to what other people are playing. If you enjoy playing with other people, you might want to think about forming a band and even playing some live gigs. Listen to other guitarists in action and see if you can buy any sheet music of their tunes. Learning what chords and melodies they use could help you to write your own songs. Spend enough time mastering the guitar and you could end up playing it professionally.

Glossary

acoustic in music, acoustic instruments do not need electric equipment to make their notes. An acoustic guitar can be played without pickups or an amplifier.

amplify to make something louder.

bass lower notes.

clef the symbol that appears at the start of each line of musical notation. It tells you how high or low the notes are.

finger style plucking the strings with all five fingers rather than using a pick.

half note a type of musical note that is equivalent to two quarter notes.

half step or **semitone** the smallest interval between notes.

improvising making up something.

interval the gap between two notes.

jack the connecting socket in an electric guitar or an amplifier. Cables are plugged into the jacks to link the equipment.

key a musical key shows the system of notes and chords that a piece of music uses as its central note or root. Keys are based on one of the notes (A to G) and can be major or minor.

magnetic field an area in which a magnetic force acts. Pickups on an electric guitar detect the movement of strings in a magnetic field and change these vibrations into notes.

major a type of key that is said to have a happy sound.

minor a type of key that is said to have a sad sound.

octave the interval between two consecutive notes with the same letter (e.g., from A to A).

oud an ancient instrument that has 11 strings and is played like a guitar.

pickups small magnets on an electric guitar that detect the vibrations of the strings and change these vibrations into musical notes.

pitch how high or low a note is.

power chords heavy-sounding chords that use the first and fifth notes of a scale. Sometimes the eight note, or octave, is also used to double up the first note.

quarter note a musical note that usually lasts for one beat in a simple bar of music.

rhythms how the beats of a piece of music are broken up.

solo when a single musician plays a part of a song while the other musicians accompany them.

time signature the two numbers, one on top of the other, that are written after the clef and show how many beats there are in a bar.

treble higher notes.

vibrate when something shakes back and forth very quickly.

vocalist someone who sings a piece of music.

whole note a type of musical note that is equivalent to four quarter notes or two half notes.

whole step or **tone** an interval between two notes that is equivalent to two half steps.

Guitar and Music Organizations

There are several organizations aimed at helping guitarists find teachers, study for exams, and gain professional knowledge.

The Guitar Foundation of America is an organization set up to provide classical guitarists with a full range of educational resources, performance opportunities, and competitions.

The American Federation of Musicians represents professional musicians across the United States and also offers advice, support, and guidance for musicians of all ages and abilities.

There are many music teachers and schools such as American Rock School in Florida that offer lessons in rock, blues, and jazz guitar. Ask at your local music store or search the Internet for lessons in your area.

Further Reading

Guitar Girl
by Sarra Manning (Turtleback, 2005)

How to Write Songs on Guitar
by Rikky Rooksby (Backbeat, 2009)

The Science of a Guitar
by Anna Claybourne (Gareth Stevens Publishing, 2009)

Web Sites

Due to the changing nature of Internet links, PowerKids Press has developed an online list of Web sites related to the subject of this book. This site is updated regularly. Please use this link to access this list:
http://www.powerkidslinks.com/mt/guitar

Index